UNIVERSITY OF MICHIGAN.

BY-LAWS

OF THE DEPARTMENT OF

SCIENCE, LITERATURE AND THE ARTS,

ADOPTED BY THE BOARD OF REGENTS, AND ORDERED PRINTED,

JUNE 25th, 1855.

ANN ARBOR:
E. B. POND, PRINTER, ARGUS OFFICE.
1855.

BY-LAWS.

CODE OF RULES AND REGULATIONS for the Government of the Department of Science, Literature and the Arts in the University of Michigan.

CHAPTER I.

OF THE FACULTY AND THEIR DUTIES.

1. The President and Professors now or hereafter appointed shall constitute the Faculty of this Department and shall be styled the Faculty of Science, Literature and the Arts.

2. The immediate government of the Department shall be vested in the Faculty, and it shall be their duty to direct and instruct the students in the several branches of learning taught in this Department, to encourage them in the acquisition of knowledge and the practice of virtue, to counsel and warn the offending, and faithfully and impartially administer the laws established by the Regents.

3. The President of the University shall preside at Commencements, Junior Exhibitions and regular meetings of the Faculty, and have power to call special meetings whenever in his judgment necessary, or upon application of any two Professors. He shall also make annually to the Regents a report upon the condition of the University.

4. At all meetings of the Faculty a majority of the acting Professors shall constitute a quorum. In the absence of the President, a President pro tem. shall be appointed by the Faculty. The presiding officer shall be always entitled to vote.

5. The Faculty shall annually appoint a Secretary who shall keep a record of all their proceedings. He shall also keep a book in which shall be registered the time of entrance, name and residence of each student, with the name and residence of his parent or guardian if a minor, and the time and circumstances of his leaving the University.

6. Any member or members of the Faculty may at any time communicate with the board of Regents, on matters pertaining to the interests of the University.

CHAPTER II.

OF THE SYSTEM OF INSTRUCTION AND EXAMINATIONS.

1. The selection of the text books used in any department shall be made by the Professor in charge of that department, but shall be liable to the revision of the Faculty and Regents.

2. The arrangement of the studies and the appointment of all the exercises connected therewith, shall be under the direction of the Faculty, liable to the revision of the Board of Regents.

3. There shall be, each term, a public examination of all the classes on the studies by them respectively pursued during the term, and note shall be taken by the several members of the Faculty, and such members of the Board of Regents as may be present, of the standing of each student, as evinced by his several examinations. At the close of the examination, the Faculty shall meet and determine by formal vote, what students shall be permitted to pass on to the studies of the next term, and no one shall so pass until he has received from the Faculty a notification of his standing, authorizing him to proceed with his class.

4. The examination upon each subject of study shall be conducted by the officer under whose direction the study was pursued.

CHAPTER III.

OF ADMISSION INTO COLLEGE.

1. Every candidate for admission shall present satisfactory evidence of good moral character, and when coming from another

collegiate institution shall exhibit a certificate of honorable dismission.

2. No candidate shall be admitted to the Freshman class under fourteen years of age, nor to any advanced standing, without a proportional advancement in age.

3. Every candidate for admission to the Freshman class shall pass an examination satisfactory to the Faculty, in the preparatory studies, as published in the last previous catalogue, and every applicant for an advanced standing shall be examined, not only in the preparatory course, but also in all the previous studies of the class which he proposes to enter.

4. Every student admitted to recitation shall be considered, by virtue of his connection with the University, as entering into an engagement to observe all the rules and regulations established for the government of the Department.

5. The course prescribed, upon his arrival, to a candidate for admission is as follows:

1st. He shall present himself, with his credentials, to the President or President pro tem., who, if he approves the applicant's papers, will return a certificate accordingly.

2d. The President's certificate shall entitle the applicant to examination by the appropriate Professors, in the required preparatory studies, upon passing which he shall receive from each examining officer a certificate accordingly.

3d. The applicant shall then present his examination certificates to the Steward, to whom he shall pay his initiation fee and other dues, and for which payment he shall receive the Steward's receipt.

4th. Upon first entering upon his recitations in each study, he shall exhibit to the Professor the Steward's receipt, which shall be evidence that he is entitled to all the privileges of the Department.

5th. As soon thereafter as requested by the President, he shall write in the Matriculation book his name and age, and the place of abode of his parent or guardian.

CHAPTER IV.

OF THE DUTIES OF STUDENTS.

1. There shall be daily morning and evening prayers at such hours as the Faculty may consider most convenient and proper, and all the students are required to be present at these religious exercises.

2. Each student is required to attend divine-worship every Sabbath, under the direction of his parent or guardian.

3. Every absence from a weekly exercise shall be considered as equivalent to *two* absences from a daily exercise.

Every deficiency in a weekly exercise shall be considered equivalent to *one* absence from a daily exercise.

Every absence from prayers shall be considered equivalent to *one* absence from a daily recitation.

Every instance of tardiness or deficiency at a daily exercise shall be reckoned at one half as much as an absence.

4. Whenever the unexcused absences, failures or tardinesses of any student shall have amounted to *five* absences from a daily exercise, his parent or guardian shall be informed of the fact, and when such account amounts to ten absences from a daily exercise, he shall be considered as dismissed by his own act.

5. Leave of absence from College prayers, church or recitations, must be obtained beforehand, otherwise a satisfactory reason for not doing so must accompany the subsequent excuse, or such excuse for said absence cannot be entertained.

6. All excuses for delinquencies shall be handed in in writing to the Faculty, at their weekly meeting, and the delinquencies of any student failing to do this shall be recorded as unexcused.

7. No student shall be excused for absence at the commencement of the term without a satisfactory reason, rendered in writing by his parent or guardian.

8. No student shall leave town during a term without obtaining permission of the President.

9. No student shall be excused to return home unless at the written request of his parent or guardian.

10. No student shall put himself under the instruction of any individual not belonging to the Faculty, without their permission.

11. No invitation shall be extended by the students to any person to deliver any public address, without the previous approbation of the Faculty.

12. No student shall be allowed to play cards, or practice any species of gambling, within the college buildings; and the drinking, or bringing to the buildings to be drunk, of any intoxicating drinks is prohibited. The possession of fire-arms or gunpowder is also forbidden.

CHAPTER V.

OF FEES, RENTS, DAMAGES AND FINES.

1. Every student, on entering college, shall be required to pay the sum of ten dollars as an initiation fee.

2. Every occupied study shall be assessed the sum of five dollars per term. Not more than two students shall be permitted to occupy the same study.

3. Every student shall, upon the first day of each term, or before the first regular meeting of the Faculty, pay to the Steward all charges made against him, or failing to do so he shall be debarred the privileges of the University. The Steward's receipt in full shall in all cases entitle the student to enter upon the exercises of his class.

4. All damages occurring to the University property shall be assessed upon the students in the manner hereinafter specified. Damages under five dollars shall be assessed by the Steward; damages over five dollars shall be assessed by the Faculty.

5. If any student or students shall have committed any willful or intentional damage, they shall be liable each to a fine of three dollars, and to any other college punishment which the Faculty may judge the circumstances of the case require.

6. Fines shall be imposed for other misdemeanors as follows:

1st. For taking up or causing to be taken up any ashes in any other receptacle than that provided by the Steward, five dollars.

2d. For carrying fire from room to room in any vessel or dish except a closed fire-pan, five dollars.

3d. For neglect to return a key at the close of the year, or upon removing from the college building, seventy-five cents.

CHAPTER VI.

OF THE LIBRARY.

1. The Librarian shall have the custody of the Library of the University, and shall suffer it to be consulted under such rules and restrictions as the President and Faculty may prescribe; and they shall be responsible to the Regents for the general management and safe keeping of the Library.

CHAPTER VII.

OF THE STEWARD AND HIS DUTIES.

1. The Regents shall appoint a Steward, who shall be the agent of the Board, and shall perform financial duties as hereinafter prescribed, and shall, within ten days of his appointment, deposite with the President of the Board satisfactory bonds for the faithful discharge of his duty, in a sum not less than five thousand dollars.

2. The duties of the Steward shall be as follows :

1st. To collect regular initiation fees, room rents, and all other moneys payable by students.

2d. To give receipts for moneys paid—to distribute the By-Laws, and to communicate to the Faculty, at each regular meeting, a list of the names of students, not previously reported, whose dues remain unpaid.

3d. To allot rooms to students and furnish them with keys.

4th. To inspect all the rooms at the beginning of every term, and keep a record in writing of their condition.

5th. To inspect all the rooms once a month; and during the season for fires, to examine the stoves, pipes and flues, and cause them to be cleaned and preserved from danger of fires.

6th. To inspect also the several buildings occupied by the resident Professors, and report forthwith to the executive committee any violation of the terms of the policy of insurance, as to the deposit of ashes or other matter endangering said buildings.

7th. To furnish fuel for the public and private rooms, and lights, when necessary, for the public rooms.

8th. To assess damages upon the students to the amount of five dollars, and under the following discriminations:

(*a*) All damages occurring in private rooms are chargeable upon the occupants, unless they designate the aggressor, or prove, to the satisfaction of the Steward, that the damage occurred without their fault.

(*b*) All damages occurring in any hall are chargeable upon the residents in that hall.

(*c*) All damages occurring in any recitation room are chargeable upon the class or classes reciting in such room.

(*d*) All damages occurring elsewhere are chargeable upon the body of students. Provided, in all cases, where the individual aggressors are known, they shall make good the damages.

9th. To assess expenses of fuel, lights for public rooms, inspections, cleaning and ordinary repairs, upon the same principles as assessment of damages.

10th. To provide for all ordinary repairs and the reparation of damages.

11th. To superintend improvements of the grounds.

12th. To exercise a general and special superintendence over the buildings and premises.

13th. To keep an accurate account of all his receipts and disbursements as well as a record of all his transactions.

14th. To present annually to the Board of Regents a report comprising,

(*a*) A detailed statement with vouchers of all his financial operations.

(*b*) A statement of the condition of the college buildings internally and externally; of the Professors residences, and of the college property generally.

(*c*) A statement and estimate of repairs and improvements which in his judgment are necessary.

(*d*) A complete inventory of the university property which is located at Ann Arbor, together with an estimate of the cost of the same.

15th. The Steward shall not suffer any repairs, additions or alterations to be made in any room of the college or appurtenances of any room except under his own direction.

16th. The Steward shall see that all rooms are vacated and closed on the day following the close of the collegiate year, and that no student has ingress during the vacation, without his consent, or remains during the vacation without the permission of the Faculty.

5. In case of the absence of the Steward or inability to discharge his duties, the President shall have power to appoint an acting steward during such interval, or until other provision shall be made by the Regents.

6. The Regents may at any time appoint a Janitor who shall be the agent and assistant of the Steward.

CHAPTER VIII.

OF DISMISSIONS, ACADEMICAL DEGREES, &c.

1. Students not minors may have at any time a dismission on their own request, and minors, on the request of their parents; provided, in either case there is no reason connected with the government of the college for refusing it.

2. In order that any student may be admitted to the degree of Bachelor of Arts, or Bachelor of Sciences, he shall have completed the course of academical exercises appointed by law for the space of four years, unless he had been admitted to an advanced standing; and on the examination to be held at the close of the studies of the senior year, or a subsequent special examination, appointed by the Faculty, he shall have been approved as a candidate for the proposed degree.

3. All candidates for any degree shall be personally present unless the Faculty shall judge it proper to confer the honor of a degree on an absent candidate.

4. The degree of Master of Arts will not be conferred in course upon graduates of three years standing, but only upon such graduates as have pursued professional or general scientific studies during that

period. The candidate for the degree shall satisfy the Faculy that he has conformed to the foregoing provision. He may also read a thesis before one of the Faculties of the University at the time of taking the degree.

5. The President shall, on the first day of the annual meeting, transmit to the Board of Regents a report, approved by a majority of the Faculty, embracing in full the name and residence of each candidate, and recommending them severally to the degree of Bachelor of Arts, or Bachelor of Sciences.

6. A similar report shall be made relative to candidates recommended to the second degree.

7. The fee for a Diploma shall be two dollars.

CHAPTER IX.

OF THE MANNER OF CONFERRING DEGREES; COMMENCEMENT, AND OTHER PUBLIC EXERCISES.

1. The degrees shall be conferred by the President, under the authority of the Board of Regents.

2. The candidates for degrees shall attend such public processions on Commencement day as the Faculty may direct, and perform such public exercises as may have been previously assigned them. The name of no student shall be presented by the Faculty to the Board of Regents for the first degree, until he has exhibited to the Faculty the receipt of the Steward for the payment of all his dues. No public exhibition or exercises, shall take place without the approval of the Faculty. A failure in either respect on the part of a candidate shall authorize the President to withold his diploma.

3. The public exercises of the day shall commence and close with prayer, and be conducted agreeably to the order prescribed by the Faculty.

www.ingramcontent.com/pod-product-compliance
Lightning Source LLC
LaVergne TN
LVHW020639110826
845149LV00004B/1280

9781418189631